The Complete Book of Jewish Rounds

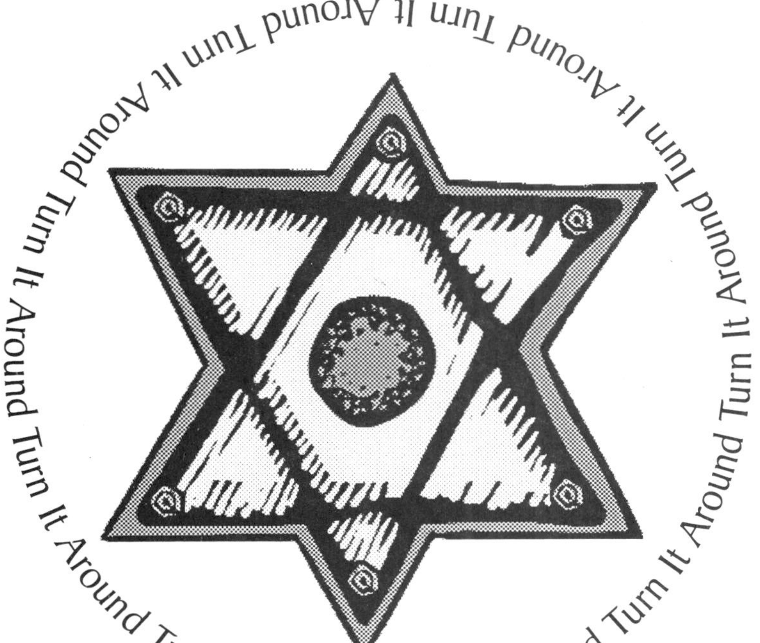

J. Mark Dunn, Editor

Transcontinent
The world's leading

Hebrew Pronunciation Guide

VOWELS	CONSONANTS
a as in f<u>a</u>ther	ch as in German Ba<u>ch</u> or Scottish lo<u>ch</u> (not as in <u>ch</u>eese)
ai as in <u>ai</u>sle (= long i as in <u>i</u>ce)	g = hard g as in get (not soft g as in gem)
e = short e as in b<u>e</u>d	tz = as in boa<u>ts</u>
ei as in <u>ei</u>ght (= long a as in <u>a</u>ce)	h after a vowel is silent
i as in p<u>i</u>zza (= long e as in b<u>e</u>)	
o = long o as in g<u>o</u>	
u = long u as in l<u>u</u>nar	
' = unstressed vowel close to ə or unstressed short e	

THE COMPLETE BOOK OF JEWISH ROUNDS: TURN IT AROUND

A Division of the Union of American Hebrew Congregations
633 Third Avenue - New York, NY 10017 - Fax 212.650.4109
212.650.4101 - www.transcontinentalmusic.com - tmp@uahc.org

Manufactured in the United States of America
Design by Joel N. Eglash
ISBN 8074-0819-
10 9 8 7 6 5 4 3 2

PREFACE

ROUNDS AND CANONS HAVE ALWAYS FASCINATED ME. They are simple in concept yet can be fiendishly difficult in execution. Their composition has occupied the minds of the world's greatest composers, and the mouths of children playing jump rope. Rounds are immediately accessible, yet, they provide a wealth of pedagogical material. This book is an attempt to make available to singers (or instrumentalists) of any age or proficiency the music of some of the best Jewish composers and songwriters. It is my hope, as choristers continue singing, that larger works by the composers represented herein will be encountered. Most of these rounds were written especially for this book; others are folk tunes, tunes gleaned from previously existing collections, and a few Renaissance contrafacta.

Besides serving as a portal into the world of Jewish music and texts, this book provides material to the conductors with which they can train their choirs in art of solid vocal technique and musicianship. There is no better way to train children and adults in the musical arts than through singing.

I hope this little book is found to be a source of challenging and meaningful repertoire for beginning choirs, and a tool by which the skills of more advanced choirs can be honed. It remains for me to express my gratitude to the composers and songwriters who graciously contributed to this book. Lastly, my thanks for the vision and work of Cantor Stephen Richards, whose Hebrew Part-Songs and Rounds was the seed from whence this little book grew. May the One who is the Master of all Song prosper the work of our hands and voices.

J. Mark Dunn, Editor
16 May 2002
Erev Shavuot, 5762

Chanukah

Psalms & Biblical Texts

Ethical Teachings

Liturgy

Other

Chanukah

Chanukah Catch

Stephen Richards

Chanukiah is the proper name for the 8-branch candlestick for *Chanukah.*

Chanukah - Festival of Lights

Sara Krohn

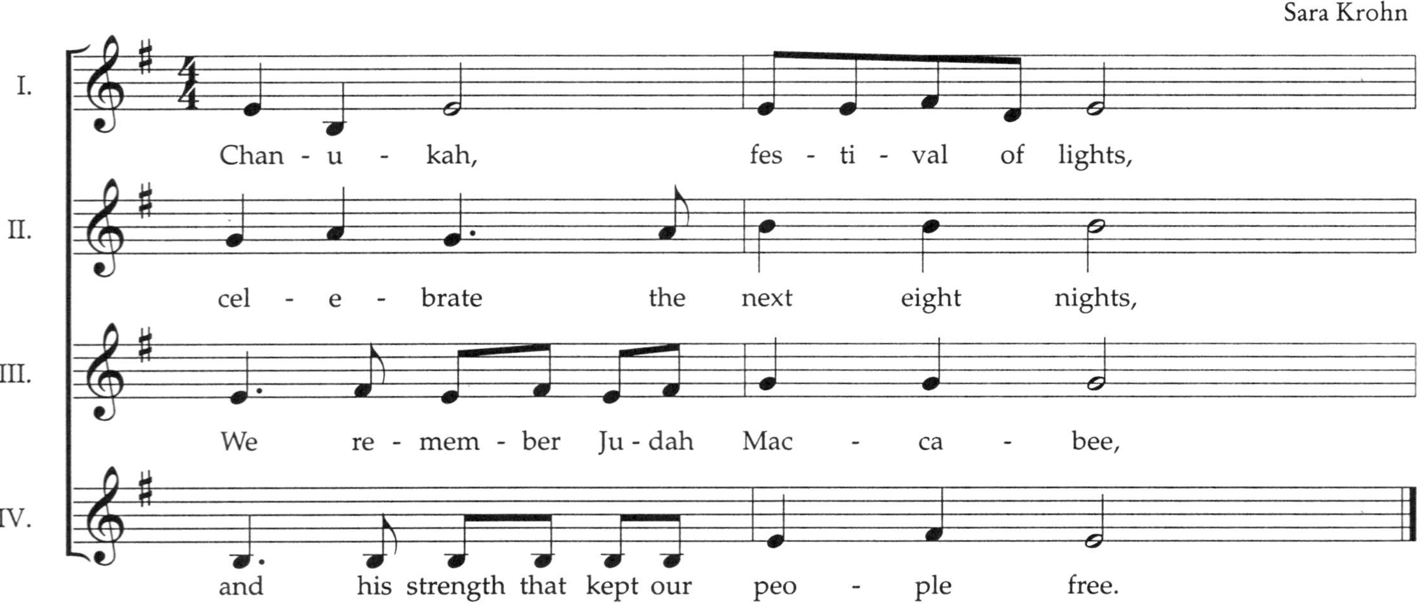

Chanukah/Solstice

Linda Hirschhorn

To facilitate readability, this canon has been printed linearly. The entries are marked I-IV.

Festival of Freedom

Ronna Honigman

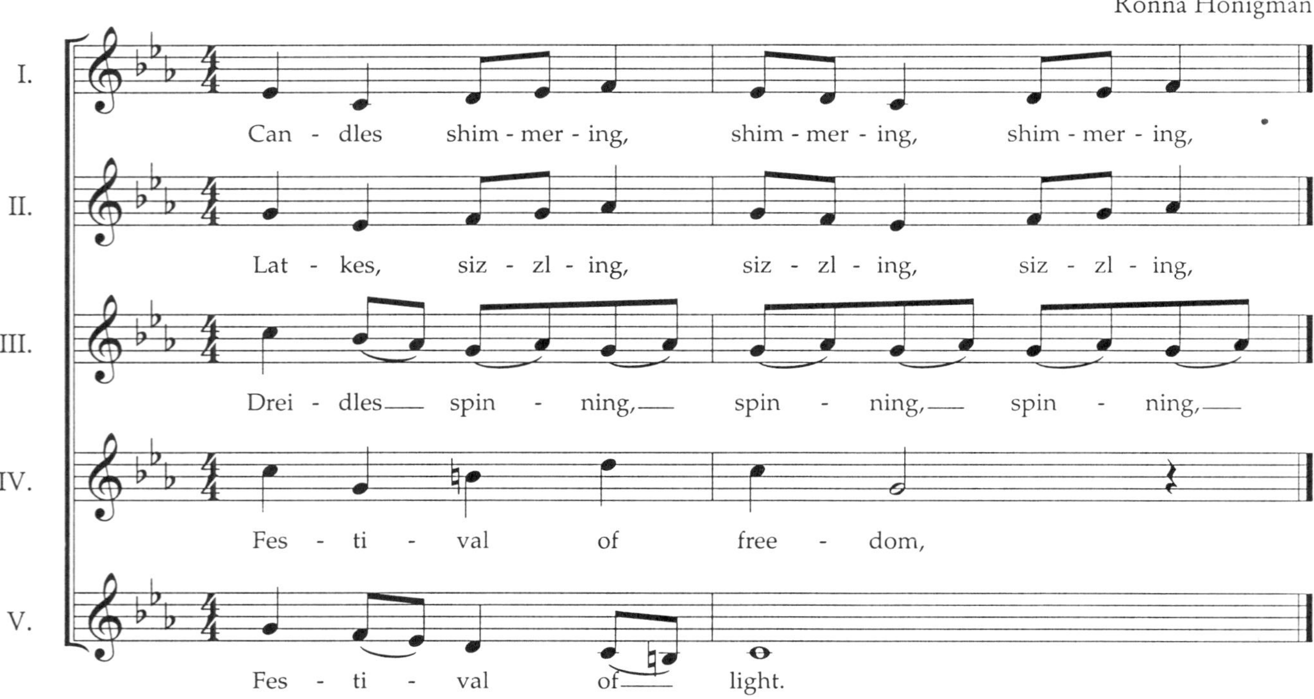

Latkes are potato pancakes, a food traditionally eaten at *Chanukah*.
Dreidles are four-sided tops used in a children's *Chanukah* game.

Judah Maccabee

Ronna Honigman

8
Let's Light the Chanukah Candles
Bonia Shur
ASCAP
Joyfully
I.
Yam bam bam bam bam bam bam ya ba bam ya ba bam yam bam bam bam
II.
Yam bam bam yam bam bam bam
I.
Yam bam bam bam bam bam bam ya ba bam ya bam bam bam
II.
Yam bam bam yam bam yam bam bam bam
I.
Let us light the Ha - nu - kah__ can - dles let us light right now right now.
II.
Let's light, let's light, let's light, let's light now.
Copyright © 2002 by Bonia Shur
3101 Clifton Ave., Cincinnati, OH 45220

Lots of Latkes

English Folk Song, arr. A. Leider

S'vivon: Hebrew for "top," also known as a *dreidle*.
Sov: Hebrew for "spin."

Once an Evil King

Harry Coopersmith

Psalms & Biblical Texts

My Voice / Koli

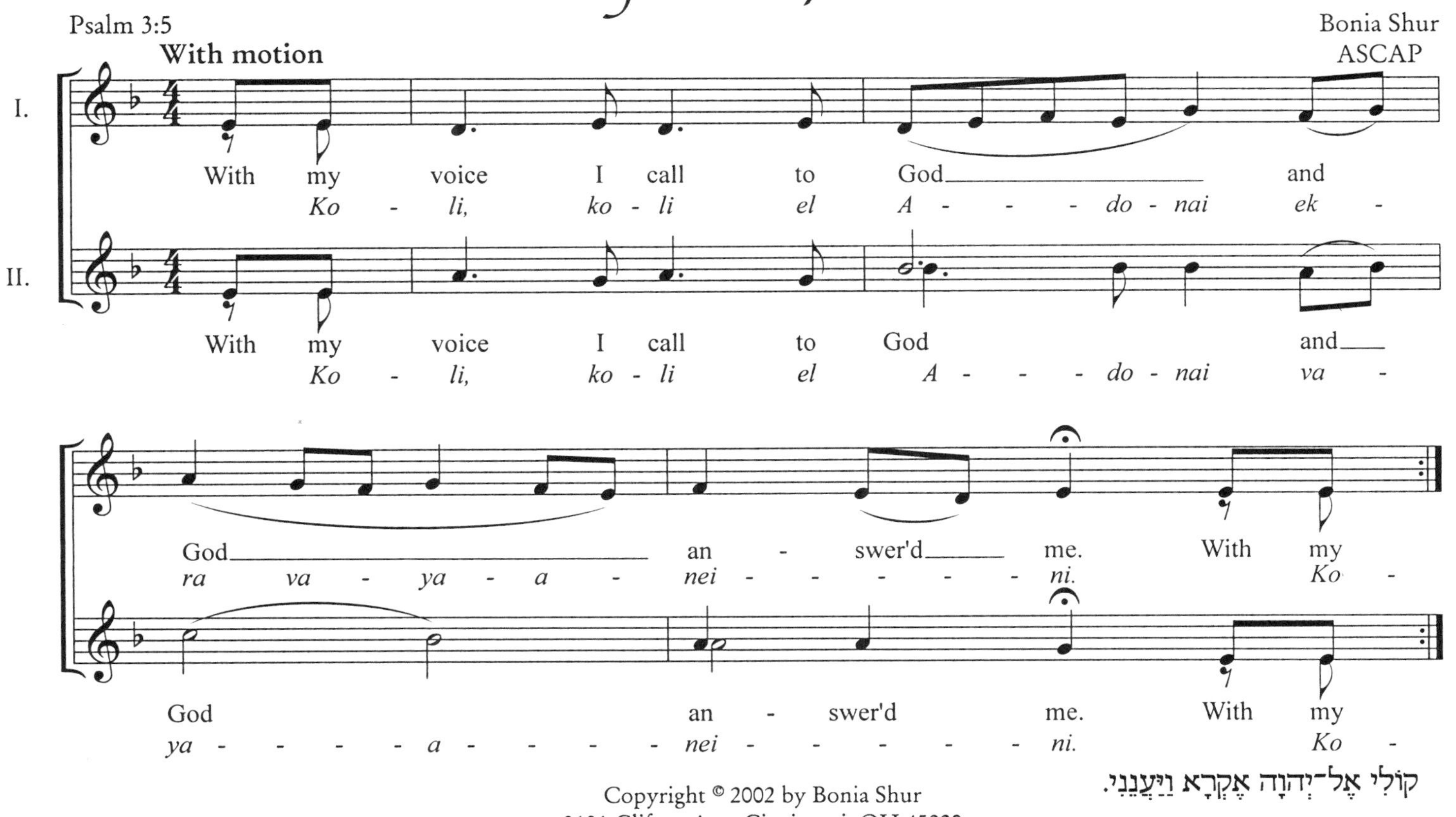

Clap Your Hands

Psalm 47:1

Bonia Shur

5
I.
(4x's)
Ah
Ah
Ah
Ah
Ah
Ah
II.
(3x's)
Ah
Ah
Ah
Ah
Ah
Ah
III.
(2x's)
Ah
Ah
Ah
Ah
Ah
Ah
IV.
(1x)
Ah
Ah
Ah
Ah
Ah
Ah
V.
Ah
Ah
Ah
Ah
Ah
Ah

I.
II.
III.
IV.
V.
f
p speak and clap
Clap
clap your hands
clap your hands
all parts together
clap your hands clap your hands clap your hands clap your hands clap your hands, your hands!

I will Give Thanks

18
fine
I.
O God a - mong the peo - ples, God.
II.
I will give thanks to You, God.
III.
and sing Your prais - - - es. God.

Shir Mizmor

Psalm 66:1-2

Bonia Shur
ASCAP

A song. A psalm.
Sing the glory of God's name

שִׁיר מִזְמוֹר הָרִיעוּ לֵאלֹהִים. זַמְּרוּ כְבוֹד־שְׁמוֹ.

May God be Gracious to Us
Psalm 67:1,2
Bonia Shur
ASCAP
Con moto ♩= 104
I.
mp
May, may God be gra - cious to us and bless us, may
II.
mp
May God be gra - cious and bless us, may
III.
mp
May, may God be be gra - cious may God bless us may
IV.
mp
be may God be gra - cious may God bless us may
V.
mp
be may God be be gra - cious may God bless us may God show us
VI.
mp
be be gra - - - cious to

I.
God show us show us fa - vor.
Se - lah.
II.
God show us show-us fa - vor.
Se - lah.
III.
God show us show us fa - - - vor.
Se - lah.
May God
IV.
God show us show us fa - - - vor.
Se - lah.
May God
V.
may God show us show show us fa - - - vor.
Se - lah.
May God
Fine
VI.
us and show us fa - vor.
Se - lah.

It is Good to Give Thanks

Psalm 92:2

Michael Horvit

I. It is good to give thanks to the Lord, to sing__ hymns to Your name,______

II. It is good to give thanks to the Lord, to sing__ hymns to Your

I. sing hymns to Your name, O Most High! It is good to give thanks to the

II. name,____________ sing hymns to Your name, O Most High! It is

Worship the Lord

Adonai Malach

Psalm 97:1

Samuel Adler

יְהֹוָה מָלָךְ תָּגֵל הָאָרֶץ יִשְׂמְחוּ אִיִּים רַבִּים.

Sing to God

Psalm 105:2

Michael Horvit

Hodu Ladonai

Psalm 118:1a

Renaissance Canon
adapted by Stephen Richards

I. Ho - du la - do - nai, Ho - du__ la - do - nai, Ho - du__ la - do -

II. nai, Ho - du la - do - nai, Ho du.

III. Ho - du, ho - du la - do - nai. Ho - du

IV. la - do - nai, Ho - du la - do - nai, ho - du la - do - nai.__

V. la - do - nai, Ho - du la - do - nai, ho - du la - do - nai.__

fine

הודו לַיְיָ.

I Will Lift Up Mine Eyes

Psalm 121:1, 2

Michael Horvit

I.
I will lift up mine eyes to the moun - tains:
II.
My help will come from the Lord, from the Lord.
III.
what is the source of my help? of my help?
I.
what is the source of my help? of my help?
II.
I will lift up mine eyes to the moun - tains:
III.
My help will come from the Lord, from the Lord.

Hineih Mah Tov

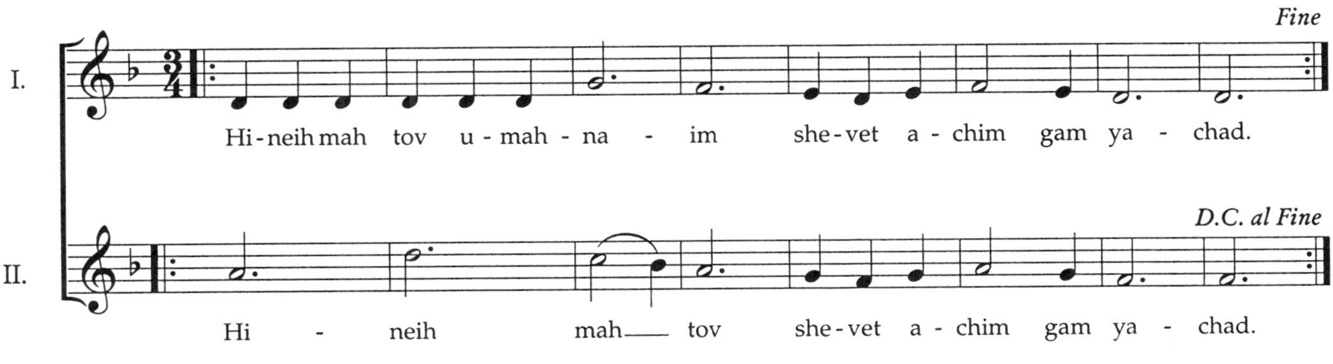

How good and pleasant it is when kin sit down together

הִנֵּה מַה־טּוֹב וּמַה־נָּעִים שֶׁבֶת אַחִים גַּם יָחַד.

Hineih Mah Tov

Psalm 133:1

Gershon Kingsley

How good and pleasant it is when kin sit down together.

הִנֵּה מַה־טּוֹב וּמַה־נָּעִים שֶׁבֶת אַחִים גַּם יָחַד.

from the composer's Shabbat Service Nashir B'yachad

I
II
III
Hi-neih mah tov u-mah-na - im she-vet a - chim gam ya - chad. Hi-neih mah tov
Hi-neih mah tov u-mah-na-im she-vet a-chim gam ya - chad.
Hi-neih mah
Hi-neih mah tov

poco legato
I
u-mah-na-im she-vet a-chim gam ya - chad. Hi-neih mah tov u - mah - na - im
poco legato
II
tov u-mah-na - im she-vet a - chim gam ya-chad. Hi-neih mah tov u-mah-na-
poco legato
III
u-mah-na-im she-vet a-chim gam ya - chad. Hi-neih mah tov

I
she-vet a-chim gam ya - chad. Hi - neih mah tov u - mah - na - im she-vet a-chim gam
II
im she-vet a - chim gam ya - chad. Hi-neih mah tov u-mah-na - im she-vet a -
III
u - mah-na-im she - vet a-chim gam ya - chad. Hi-neih mah tov u - mah-na - im

I
ya - chad. Hi - neih mah tov u - mah - na - im she - vet a - chim gam ya - chad.
II
chim gam ya - chad. Hi - neih mah tov u - mah - na - im she - vet a - chim gam ya - chad.
III
she - vet a - chim gam ya - chad. She - vet a - chim gam ya - chad, gam ya - chad.

Unison all the way through.
Repeat as four-part canon *(D.C.al Coda)*

Psalm 150

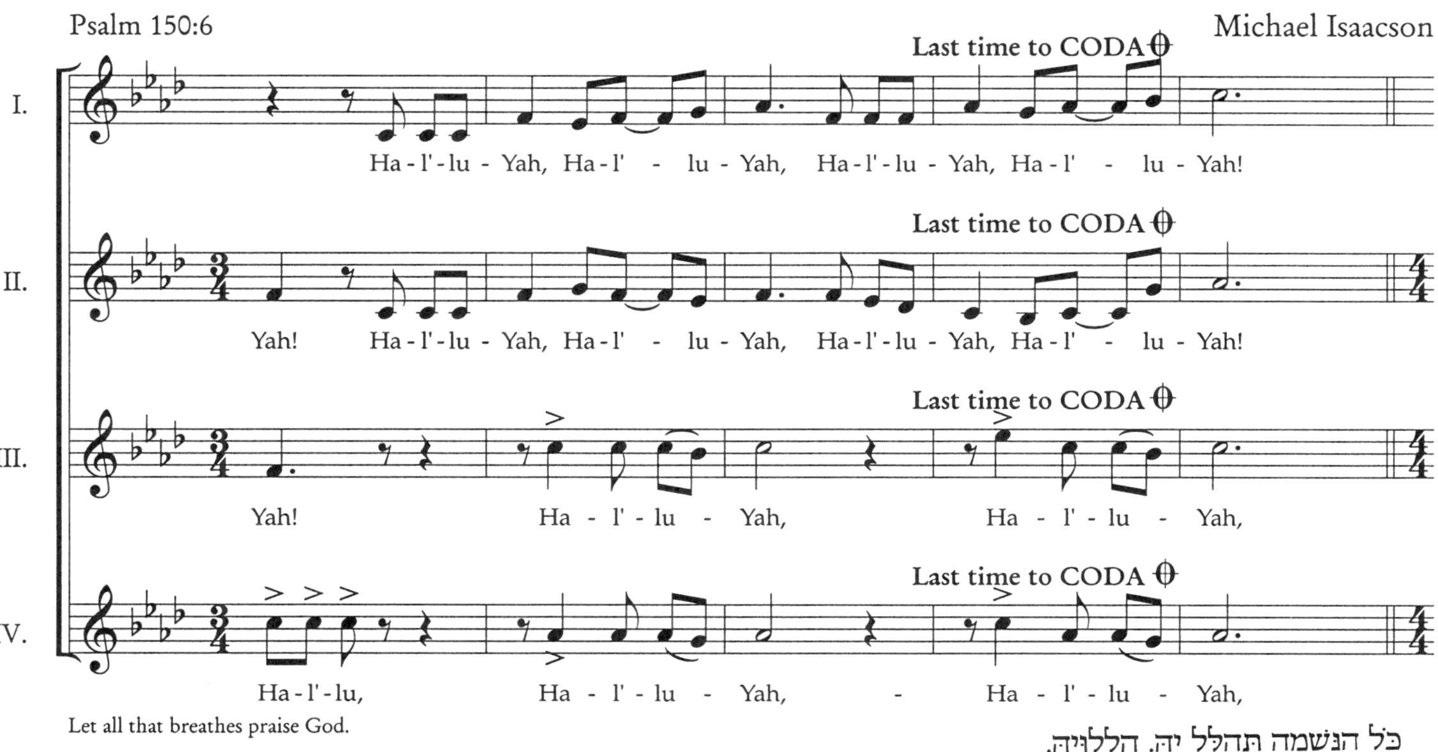

36
Kol han'-sha-mah t'-ha-leil-Yah, Ha-l'-lu-Yah, Ha-l'-lu-
Kol han'-sha-mah t'-ha-leil-Yah, Ha-l'-lu-Yah, Ha-l'-lu-
Ha-l'-lu-Yah, Ha-l'-lu-Yah!
Ha-l'-lu-Yah, Ha-l'-lu-Yah!
CODA
I & III
II & IV
Unison
Yah! Kol han'-sha-mah Kol han'-sha-mah t'-ha-leil-Yah, Ha-l'-lu, -Yah!

Kol Han'shamah

Psalm 150: 6

Michael Praetorius
adapted by Stephen Richards

כֹּל הַנְּשָׁמָה תְּהַלֵּל יָהּ. הַלְלוּיָהּ.

Mi Zot Olah

Who is she that comes from the desert
like columns of smoke and frankincense?

מִי זֹאת עֹלָה מִן־הַמִּדְבָּר? כְּתִימְרוֹת עָשָׁן.
מְקֻטֶּרֶת מוֹר וּלְבוֹנָה. אֲנִי לְדוֹדִי וְדוֹדִי לִי.

Yavo Dodi

Let my beloved come to his garden
and enjoy its luscious fruits!

יָבֹא דוֹדִי לְגַנּוֹ וְיֹאכַל פְּרִי מְגָדָיו.

Ani L'Dodi

Song of Songs 6:3

Bonia Shur
ASCAP

I am my beloved's
and my beloved is mine;
he browses among the lilies.

אֲנִי לְדוֹדִי וְדוֹדִי לִי הָרֹעֶה בַּשּׁוֹשַׁנִּים.

A TIME

Ecclesiastes 3:8

Bonia Shur (ASCAP)

עֵת לִבְכּוֹת וְעֵת לִשְׂחוֹק.
עֵת מִלְחָמָה וְעֵת שָׁלוֹם.

Ethical Teachings

Amar Rabbi Akivah

Sifra
Leviticus 19:18

Ronna Honigman

Rabbi Akiva said: "Love your neighbor as yourself."

אָמַר רַבִּי אֲקִיבָה: וְאָהַבְתָּ
לְרֵעֲךָ כָּמוֹךָ.

If I am Not for Myself

Pirkei Avot 1, 14

Gershon Kingsley

Solo or Unison

I.

f

If I am not for my - self, who will be for me?

5

I.

If I am not for my - self, who will be for me? Yet if I am for my - self a - lone, of what good am

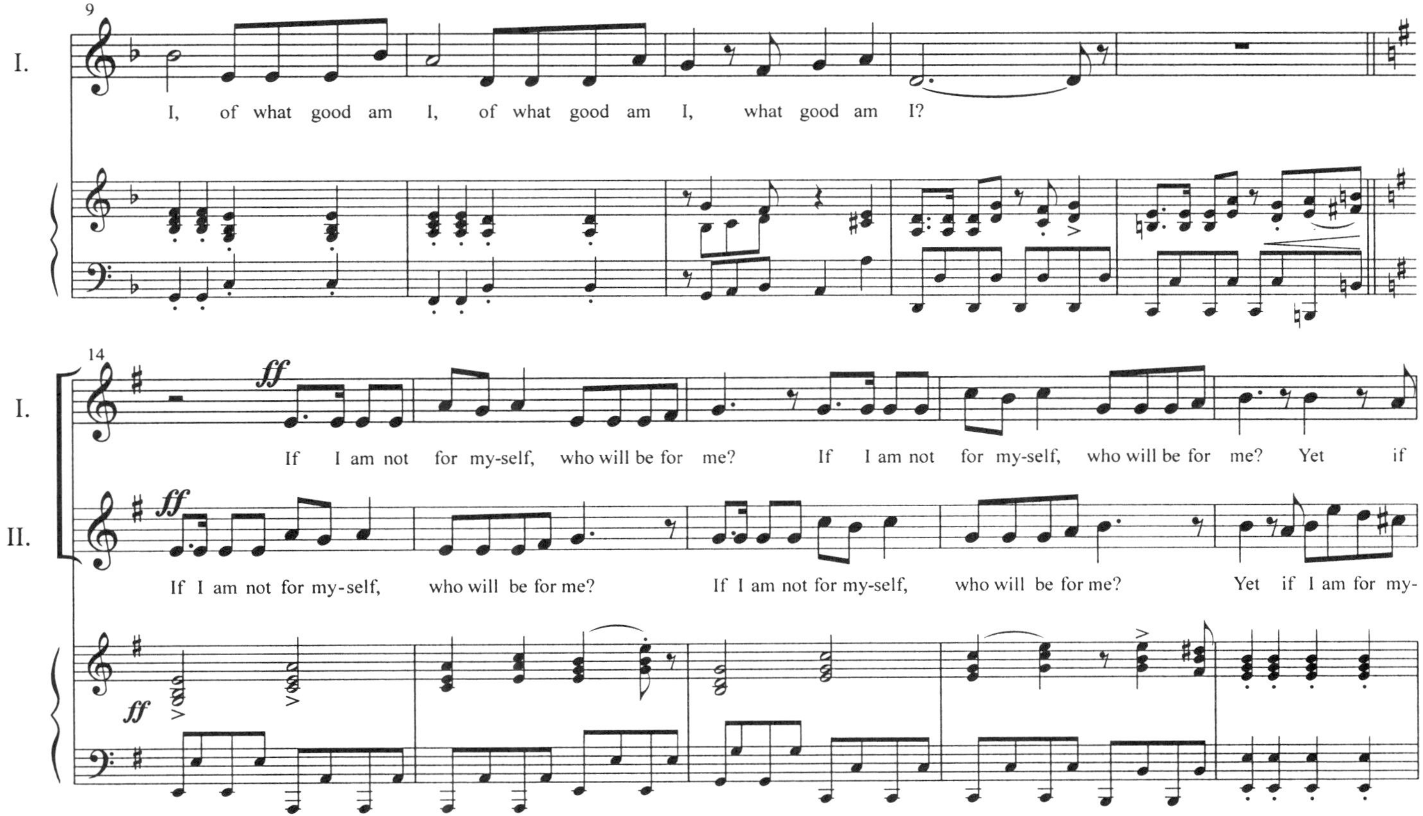

9

I. I, of what good am I, of what good am I, what good am I?

14

I. If I am not for my-self, who will be for me? If I am not for my-self, who will be for me? Yet if

II. If I am not for my-self, who will be for me? If I am not for my-self, who will be for me? Yet if I am for my-

19
I.
I am for my-self a-lone, of what good am I, of what good am I, of what good am I, what
II.
self a-lone, of what good am I, of what good am I, of what good am I, what good am
23
I.
good am I? what good am I, what good am I, what good am I?
II.
I? what good am I, what good am I, what good am I, am I?

For Ari and Andy Isaacson

Help!

Inspired by Ethics of the Fathers
Pirkei Avot 2.6

Michael Isaacson

[Hillel said:] "In a place where no one behaves
like a human being, you must strive to be human."

For Melissa, Nolan, and Zachary Goldberg

Turn It Around

Inspired by Ethics of the Fathers
Pirkei Avot 5,22

Michael Isaacson

Ben Bag Bag said: "Turn it [the Torah] over and over again, for it contains everything in it. Keep your eyes riveted to it.

Hillel Omer

Pirkei Avot 2:4

Laura Berkson

Hillel said: "Do not separate yourself from the community, and don't judge your fellow human being until you have reached that persons place."

הִלֵּל אוֹמֵר: אַל תִּפְרֹשׁ מִן הַצִּבּוּר;
וְאַל תָּדִין אֶת־חֲבֵרְךָ עַד
שֶׁתַּגִּיעַ לִמְקוֹמוֹ.

Liturgy

Adon Olam

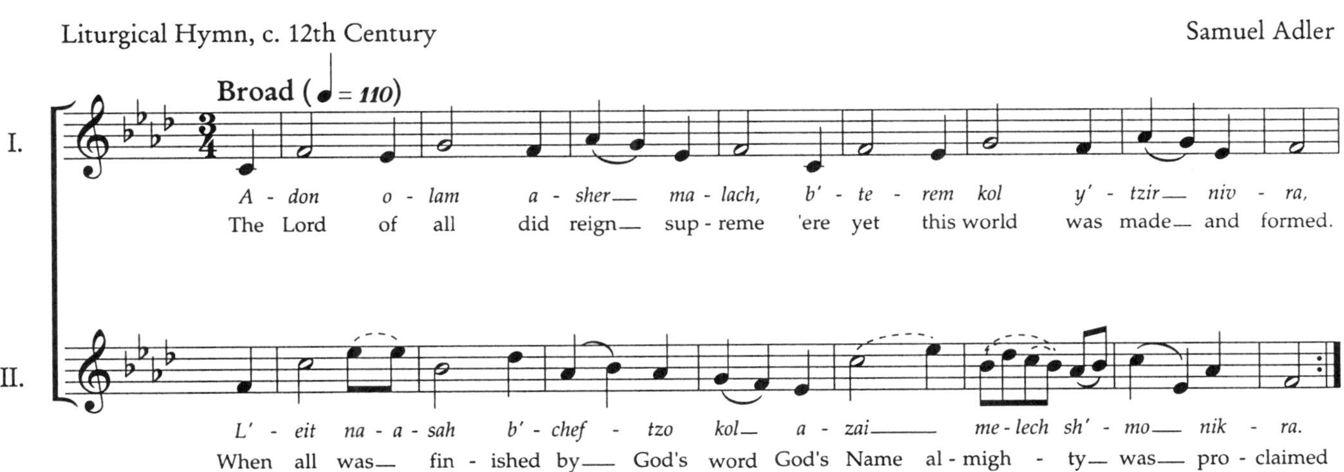

אֲדוֹן עוֹלָם, אֲשֶׁר מָלַךְ, בְּטֶרֶם כָּל־יְצִיר נִבְרָא,
לְעֵת נַעֲשָׂה בְחֶפְצוֹ כֹּל, אֲזַי מֶלֶךְ שְׁמוֹ נִקְרָא.

Ashrei

Morning Liturgy
Psalm 84:5

Samuel Adler

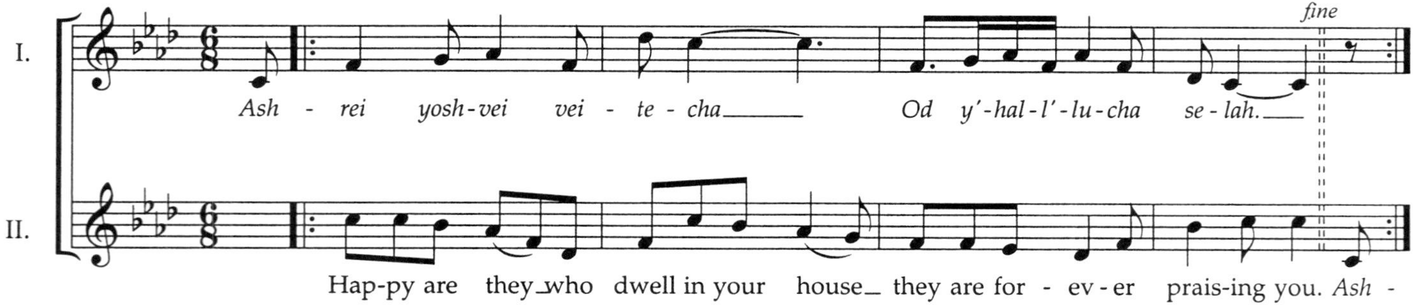

I.

fine

Ash - rei yosh-vei vei - te - cha____ Od y'-hal-l'-lu-cha se - lah.___

II.

Hap-py are they‿who dwell in your house‿ they are for - ev - er prais-ing you. *Ash -*

אַשְׁרֵי יוֹשְׁבֵי בֵיתֶךָ עוֹד יְהַלְלוּךָ סֶּלָה.

Hashiveinu

Lamantations 5:21

Folk Tune

Turn us to you, O God, and we shall return.
Renew our days as of old.

הֲשִׁיבֵנוּ, יְיָ, אֵלֶיךָ וְנָשׁוּבָה; חַדֵּשׁ יָמֵינוּ כְּקֶדֶם.

Havdalah Round

Laura Berkson

Hodo Al Eretz

Psalm 148:13b, 14

Andrea Jill Higgins

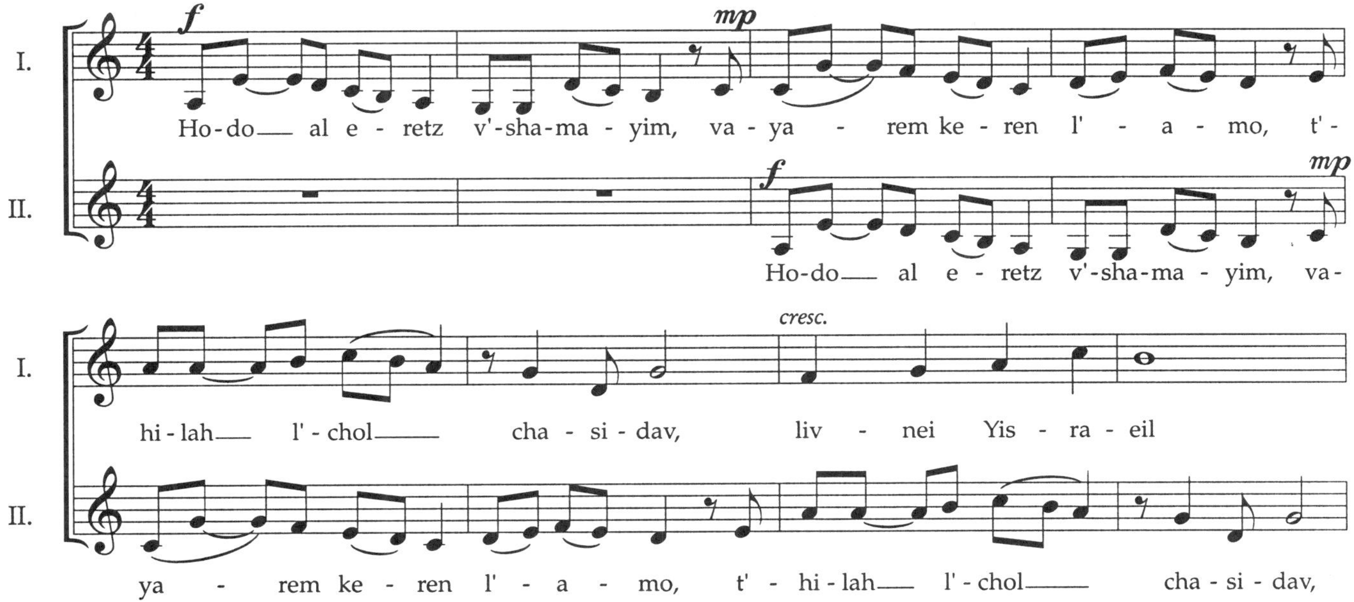

I. Ho-do — al e - retz v'-sha-ma - yim, va - ya - rem ke - ren l' - a - mo, t'-

II. Ho-do — al e - retz v'-sha-ma - yim, va-

I. hi - lah — l' - chol — cha - si - dav, liv - nei Yis - ra - eil

II. ya - rem ke - ren l' - a - mo, t' - hi - lah — l' - chol — cha - si - dav,

God's splendor covers heaven and earth
God has exalted the horn of his people to the glory of Israel
God's faithful and close ones. Hal'luyah!

הודו עַל אֶרֶץ וְשָׁמָיִם, וַיָּרֶם קֶרֶן לְעַמּוֹ,
תְּהִלָּה לְכָל־חֲסִידָיו, לִבְנֵי יִשְׂרָאֵל
עַם קְרֹבוֹ. הַלְלוּיָהּ!

I.
am k' - ro - vo. Ha - l' - lu - yah, ha - l' - lu - yah, ha - l' - lu -
II.
cresc.
liv - nei Yis - ra - eil am k' - ro - vo. Ha - l' - lu -

I.
yah, ha - l' - lu - yah.
II.
yah, ha - l' - lu - yah, ha - l' - lu - yah, ha - l' - lu - yah.

Let Us Have Songs
Ilu Finu

Morning Liturgy

Linda Hirschhorn

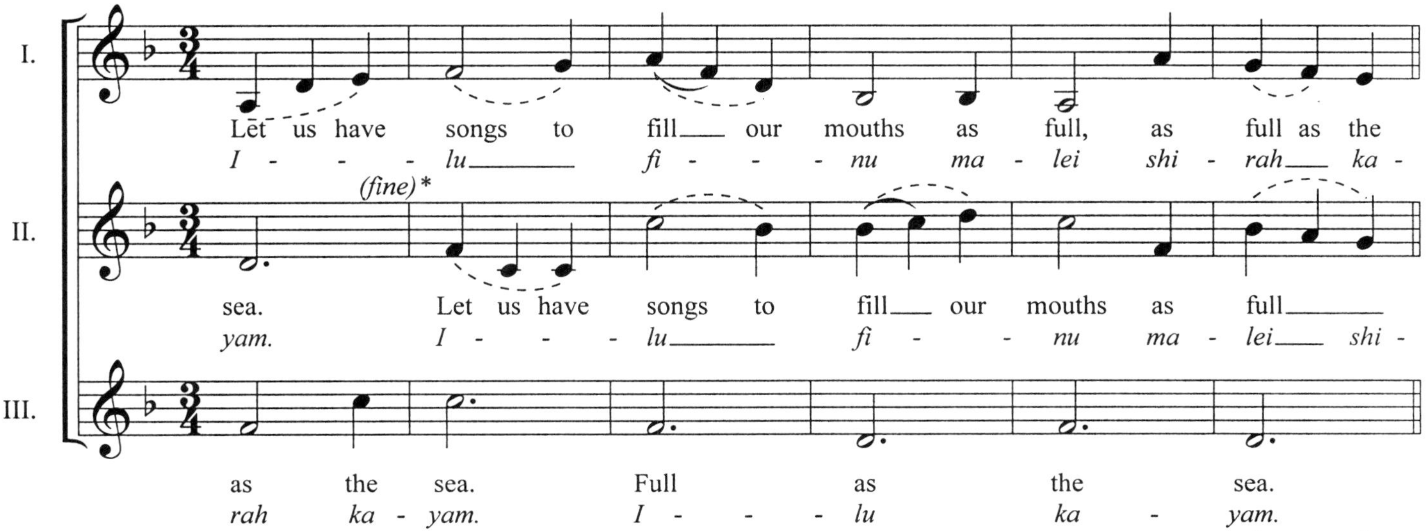

I.
Let us have songs to fill__ our mouths as full, as full as the
I - - - lu____ fi - - - nu ma - lei shi - rah__ ka -

*(fine)**

II.
sea. Let us have songs to fill__ our mouths as full____
yam. I - - - lu____ fi - - nu ma - lei__ shi -

III.
as the sea. Full as the sea.
rah ka - yam. I - - - lu ka - yam.

* As there is no convenient place to end this round, it is suggested that each part re-sing the first line as far as the *fine*, all finishing in *unison*.

אִלּוּ פִינוּ מָלֵא שִׁירָה כַּיָּם.

Mah Tovu

Numbers 24:5

composer unknown

How lovely are your tents, O Jacob,
your dwelling-places, O Israel.

מַה־טֹּבוּ אֹהָלֶיךָ, יַעֲקֹב מִשְׁכְּנֹתֶיךָ, יִשְׂרָאֵל!

Oseh Shalom

May the One who makes peace on high let peace descend upon us, Israel, and the whole world. And let us say: Amen.

עֹשֶׂה שָׁלוֹם בִּמְרוֹמָיו, הוּא יַעֲשֶׂה שָׁלוֹם
עָלֵינוּ וְעַל כָּל־יִשְׂרָאֵל, וְאִמְרוּ: אָמֵן.

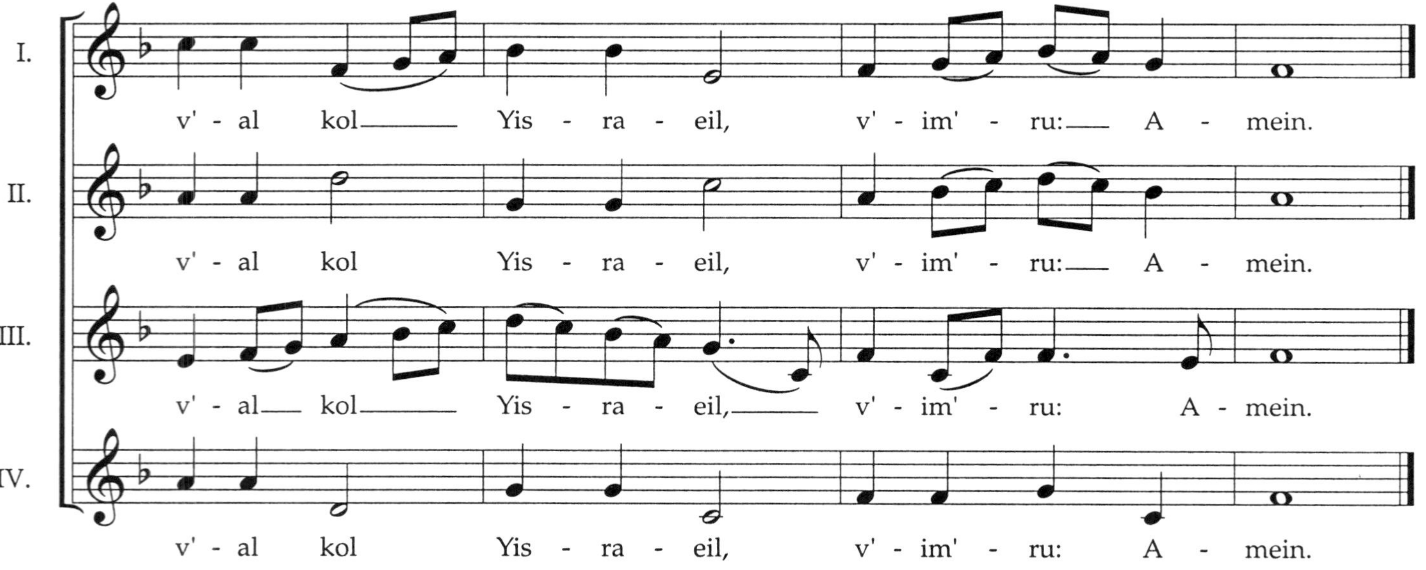
I.
v' - al kol Yis - ra - eil, v' - im' - ru: A - mein.
II.
v' - al kol Yis - ra - eil, v' - im' - ru: A - mein.
III.
v' - al kol Yis - ra - eil, v' - im' - ru: A - mein.
IV.
v' - al kol Yis - ra - eil, v' - im' - ru: A - mein.

Renaissance Canon, adapted
by Stephen Richards

I. *mf* Sha - lom, sha - lom a - lei - chem. *fine*

II. Sha - lom, sha - lom a - lei - chem. *fine*

III. Sha - lom, sha - lom a - lei - chem. *fine*

IV. Sha - lom a - lei - chem, sha - lom a - lei - chem. *fine*

V. Sha - lom a - lei - chem, sha - lom, sha - lom a - lei - chem. *fine*
last time *a - lei - chem.*

Peace to you.

שָׁלוֹם עֲלֵיכֶם!

שְׁמַע יִשְׂרָאֵל: יְיָ אֱלֹהֵינוּ, יְיָ אֶחָד!

Sim Shalom

Morning Liturgy

Chassidic

Grant peace, goodness, and blessing in the world,
grace, love, and mercy over us and all people.

שִׂים שָׁלוֹם, טוֹבָה וּבְרָכָה חֵן וָחֶסֶד וְרַחֲמִים,
עָלֵינוּ וְעַל־כָּל־יִשְׂרָאֵל עַמֶּךָ.

Dedicated to Zachari Shapiro

Yih'yu L'ratzon

Psalm 19:15

Bonia Shur
ASCAP

יְהִיוּ לְרָצוֹן אִמְרֵי־פִי וְהֶגְיוֹן לִבִּי לְפָנֶיךָ,
יְיָ, צוּרִי וְגוֹאֲלִי.

Yotzeir Or

a canon in four parts

Morning Liturgy

Laura Berkson

Blessed is our God, ruler of the universe,
who makes light and creates darkness,
who ordains peace and fashions all things.

בָּרוּךְ אַתָּה יְיָ, אֱלֹהֵינוּ מֶלֶךְ הָעוֹלָם,
יוֹצֵר אוֹר וּבוֹרֵא חֹשֶׁךְ, עֹשֶׂה שָׁלוֹם וּבוֹרֵא אֶת־הַכֹּל.

Other

Eretz Zavat Chalav

A land flowing with milk and honey.

אֶרֶץ זָבַת חָלָב וּדְבָשׁ.

Nigun

Linda Hirschhorn

Bonia Shur
ASCAP

Zum Gali Gali

Israeli Folk Song

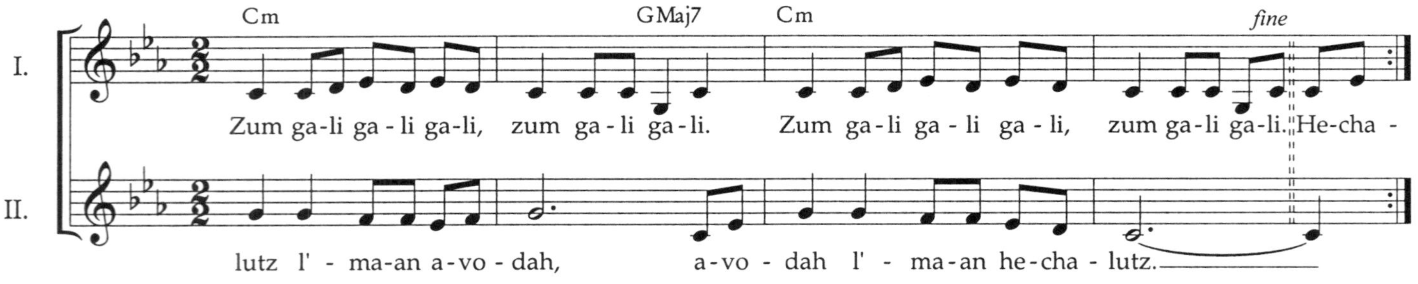

The pioneer is for the work, and the work is for the pioneer.

זוּם גַּלִּי גַּלִּי גַּלִּי, זוּם גַּלִּי גַּלִּי.
הֶחָלוּץ לְמַעַן עֲבוֹדָה, עֲבוֹדָה לְמַעַן הֶחָלוּץ.

Index By Composer

From the Editor..

• Sight singing exercises of every level of difficulty can be found in the world of the round and canon. Whether you use Solfeggio (movable or fixed Doh,) or Numbers, a great deal of mileage can be gotten from the simplest of rounds. Less difficult, two-part rounds are a good place to find exercises to drill intervallic recognition, and note duration. The more complicated are especially useful for teaching complex rhythm patterns, omitting pitch altogether and concentrating on the components of rhythm. Count singing—singing the rhythmic structure instead of the printed text—is an effective way of joining pitch and duration: ONE and TWO and-a TEE-e-and-a FOUR. Resist the temptation to play parts, especially in sight-singing exercises. It does no one any good. Allowing your choir to figure it out on their own makes musicians of your choristers, not simply followers.

• Unison singing, which is often the thing that even the best choirs do poorly, is addressed during the initial learning of the round or canon. It is at this stage that uniform vowels, crisply aligned consonants, and correct pitches and their durations are most easily addressed. This is the first stage of building a sense of "choral hearing," that is being able to hear one's self as a component of the whole choir, and make evaluations as to how effectively the one contributes the many. To put it succinctly, if a person cannot hear that his final "T" is late, no amount of lecturing on the part of the conductor will help. Only by being taught how to hear mistakes can choristers learn how and what they need to do to fix them. These rudimentary elements of choral singing are most easily taught, not by singing in parts, but by singing in unison.

• Part singing can be difficult to teach a choir, regardless of the ages of its members. Rounds offer a uniquely engaging and unthreatening way of introducing part singing. The notion of the more the better is best discarded at this point. If the round is in six parts, sing it in two parts until both groups are comfortable and accurate. If one group has a problem with a particular interval or rhythm, take the round back to unison and work on the problem, then back to parts. Be patient; singing beautifully in two parts is far more enjoyable for the choir (and for the conductor) than muddling through in six.

A higher level of "choral hearing" is attained through part-singing. Choristers must listen not only to their own line, but to the sonorities created by the presence of other parts. Now the vowels, consonants, and rhythms taught earlier in unison become imperatives for good tuning, accuracy, and precision. How many times have rounds gone wrong because of clipped beats and early entries? Count singing is an effective tool to instill rhythmic stability.

• Joyful singing really is the only way to sing. Whether or not these rounds are heard by anyone else besides the choir itself should not diminish the singular joy of singing them, and singing them well. The confidence and pride gained through a well-executed round or canon cannot help but spill over into the remainder of the rehearsal, and engender a more spirited singing in performance.